Ben Stokes

BEN STOKES: A BIOGRAPHY OF GRIT, GLORY, AND TRIUMPH

Stacy B. Russell

Ben Stokes

All rights reserved. No part of this publication may be reproduced, distributed, or transmitted in any form or by any means, including photocopying, recording, and other electronic or mechanical methods, without prior written permission of the publisher, except in case of briefs quotation embodied in critical reviews and certain other noncommercial uses permitted by copyright law.

Copyright © STACY B. RUSSELL, 2024.

Ben Stokes

TABLE OF CONTENTS

INTRODUCTION

CHAPTER ONE: WHO IS BEN STOKES?

CHAPTER TWO: EARLY LIFE AND BEGINNINGS

CHAPTER THREE: THE EARLY YEARS IN COUNTY CRICKET

CHAPTER FOUR: THE INTERNATIONAL BREAKTHROUGH

CHAPTER FIVE: THE 2019 WORLD CUP AND THE REBIRTH OF A CHAMPION

CHAPTER SIX: A LEGACY DEFINED

CHAPTER SEVEN: THE TRIALS AND TRIUMPHS

CHAPTER EIGHT: A LEGACY IN THE MAKING

CHAPTER NINE: THE PINNACLE OF SUCCESS

CHAPTER TEN: THE WEIGHT OF EXPECTATIONS

CHAPTER ELEVEN: THE LEGACY BEGINS TO FORM

Ben Stokes

INTRODUCTION

Ben Stokes is not just a name etched in cricket's record books; he is a symbol of resilience, passion, and an indomitable spirit that has captured the imagination of fans worldwide. From the streets of Christchurch to the pinnacle of international cricket, Stokes' journey has been anything but conventional. His story is one of grit, determination, and overcoming personal and professional challenges that would have derailed most athletes. It's a story that goes beyond the boundaries of the cricket field and delves into the heart of what it means to be human, to rise, fall, and rise again.

In a sport steeped in tradition, where the weight of history and expectations can often crush players, Stokes has emerged as a breath of fresh air. His approach to the game is fearless, his style electrifying, and his ability to produce moments of brilliance in the most intense situations is unparalleled. From his unforgettable match-winning knock in the 2019 World Cup final to his

Ben Stokes

heroic innings in the Ashes series, Stokes has consistently delivered when it mattered most, cementing his place as one of the greatest all-rounders of the modern era.

But behind the headlines and the accolades lies a complex figure, one who has battled his own demons, faced intense scrutiny, and, at times, stood at the crossroads of controversy. Stokes' life off the field has been as turbulent as his career has been dazzling. From personal struggles with mental health to navigating the intense pressures of being in the public eye, he has shown an honesty and vulnerability that has endeared him to fans and humanized the larger-than-life persona he often carries on the cricket field.

This biography aims to go beyond the statistics and the highlights, to explore the man behind the myth. Who is Ben Stokes when the cameras aren't rolling, when the stadiums are empty, and the roar of the crowd fades away? What drives him to keep pushing, to keep fighting, even when the odds are stacked against him?

Ben Stokes

How has he balanced the incredible highs with the crushing lows, and what lessons can we learn from his journey?

We will delve into the formative years that shaped him, from his early days in New Zealand to his rise through the ranks of English cricket. We'll explore the pivotal moments of his career, the triumphs, the controversies, and the times when it seemed everything was slipping away, only for him to come back stronger. Through it all, we'll uncover the qualities that make Stokes not just a great cricketer, but a symbol of perseverance and resilience in the face of adversity.

This is the story of Ben Stokes: a biography of grit, glory, and triumph. It's a story that transcends sport, offering insights into the human spirit, and showing us that true greatness isn't just about talent, it's about heart, determination, and the will to rise, again and again.

Ben Stokes

CHAPTER ONE: WHO IS BEN STOKES?

Ben Stokes is a professional cricketer known for his exceptional skill, leadership, and resilience. Born on June 4, 1991, in Christchurch, New Zealand, he moved to England at a young age, where he developed a passion for cricket. Stokes comes from an athletic family, his father, Gerard Stokes, was a rugby league player and coach, which likely influenced Ben's early involvement in sports.

Standing out for his all-round capabilities, Stokes plays as a left-handed batsman and a right-arm fast-medium bowler. His natural talent, combined with a fiercely competitive spirit, helped him make rapid progress through England's cricket ranks. He represents England in all formats of the game and has played a key role in several of the national team's most significant moments.

Ben Stokes

Known for his tenacity, charisma, and work ethic, Ben Stokes is often described as a fighter both on and off the field. His persona exudes confidence, and he has a reputation for being mentally tough, which has helped him navigate various personal and professional challenges. Stokes is not just defined by his cricketing ability, but also by his approach to the game, fearless, aggressive, and passionate, traits that have made him a fan favorite and an influential figure in English cricket.

Off the field, Stokes has experienced his share of controversies and setbacks, but his journey has also been one of growth and maturity, showing that he is more than just a cricketer, he's a resilient and multifaceted individual.

CHAPTER TWO: EARLY LIFE AND BEGINNINGS

Ben Stokes was born on June 4, 1991, in Christchurch, New Zealand, to Gerard and Deborah Stokes. His father, Gerard, was a well-known rugby league player and coach, which meant that sports were a central part of family life from the beginning. Ben grew up in a household where athletic achievement was valued, and it wasn't long before he too displayed a natural aptitude for sports. However, while his father excelled in rugby, Ben found his passion in cricket, a sport that would eventually become his life's calling.

When Ben was just 12 years old, the Stokes family relocated from New Zealand to the town of Cockermouth in England's Lake District. This move was prompted by his father's appointment as head coach of the local rugby league team. It was a significant change for young Ben, but it was in this rural English setting that his cricketing potential began to take root. Despite the challenges of adjusting to a new environment, Ben immersed himself in the sport, joining Cockermouth Cricket Club. His enthusiasm for the game was unmistakable, and it quickly became apparent that he had exceptional talent.

Stokes attended Cockermouth School, where his sporting prowess extended beyond cricket. He was a competitive swimmer and participated in various other athletic activities, further honing his physical skills. Yet, cricket remained his primary passion. It was during his teenage years that his abilities as an all-rounder started to attract attention. His powerful batting, combined with his fast-medium bowling, set him apart from his peers. Even at a young age, Ben had a natural flair for the game and displayed a work ethic that would later define his professional career.

While Cockermouth is a quiet, relatively isolated town, Ben's performances in local cricket competitions soon started to make waves beyond the small community. His natural aggression on the field, coupled with an ability to

Ben Stokes

read the game, marked him as a standout prospect. He played an important role in helping Cockermouth Cricket Club win the North Lancashire & Cumbria Cricket League Premier Division title, an achievement that cemented his reputation as a rising star.

Stokes' rapid development was not just a product of natural talent; his drive to improve and his commitment to the game were clear even at this young age. He spent countless hours in practice, often staying back after team training sessions to work on his skills. This relentless dedication to the sport would come to define his career, as Stokes was not content with being merely talented, he wanted to be the best.

By the age of 15, Ben Stokes' cricketing ability had caught the attention of scouts from higher-level teams. His first major breakthrough came when he was selected to play for the Durham Academy, one of the leading cricket development programs in England. This opportunity marked the beginning of his professional journey, giving him access to top-tier coaching and facilities. At Durham, Stokes continued to sharpen his skills, quickly rising through the ranks of youth cricket. His all-round abilities made him a valuable asset, and it became clear to everyone around him that he had the potential to reach the very highest levels of the game.

Stokes' upbringing, particularly his father's influence, played a crucial role in shaping his mindset and approach to sports. Gerard Stokes was known for his tough, no-nonsense attitude as a rugby coach, and he instilled in Ben the importance of resilience, discipline, and mental toughness. These values would serve Ben well as he embarked on a professional cricketing career that, while filled with moments of glory, would also test him in ways that few could have anticipated.

Ben's early years were not without their challenges. Moving to a new country at such a formative age, adjusting to new social environments, and living up to the expectations placed on him as the son of a prominent sports figure were pressures that he had to navigate. However, these experiences also helped shape his character, giving him the grit and determination that would later become hallmarks of his playing style.

Stokes' journey from a small-town cricket club in Cockermouth to the international stage is a testament to his hard work, commitment, and the strong support system provided by his family. Though his early life was relatively modest, his rise through the ranks of English cricket was anything but ordinary. Ben Stokes was not just a boy with a natural gift for cricket, he was a young athlete who was willing to put in the effort, overcome obstacles, and rise to the challenges that came his way. These formative years laid the foundation for the remarkable career that would follow, setting the stage for Stokes to become one of the most celebrated cricketers of his generation.

CHAPTER THREE: THE EARLY YEARS IN COUNTY CRICKET

When Ben Stokes made his transition from youth cricket to the professional ranks, it marked the beginning of a new chapter in his life, one where raw talent would be molded into a force capable of dominating at the highest level of the game. The early years of his professional career were filled with challenges, triumphs, and lessons that would shape him as both a player and a person. While the world of county cricket may seem like a step down from the international glamour of the sport, it was here, in the crucible of English domestic cricket, that Stokes' talent would truly be unleashed.

Stokes first entered the spotlight when he was picked up by Durham County Cricket Club's Academy, one of the most prestigious programs for young cricketers in England. Durham had a reputation for producing top-quality players, and the opportunity to play for a county side of such stature was a massive step forward

Ben Stokes

for Stokes. At the time, Durham was competing in the County Championship, one of the oldest and most respected cricket competitions in the world. For Stokes, the chance to train alongside seasoned professionals and test his skills against experienced opponents was invaluable.

From the outset, it was clear that Ben Stokes was a special talent. As a 17-year-old, he had the physicality, skill, and mental sharpness that belied his age. He wasn't content to merely occupy a spot in the team, he wanted to make an impact. His performances in Durham's second XI were nothing short of spectacular. Stokes quickly established himself as an all-rounder who could contribute with both bat and ball, showing an aggressive style of play that drew attention from coaches and selectors alike.

Stokes' bowling was particularly impressive during his early years at Durham. While his batting would later become one of his most famous attributes, it was his ability to bowl fast and swing the ball that initially set

Ben Stokes

him apart. He was capable of bowling at speeds that unsettled opposition batsmen, and his aggressive approach on the field earned him a reputation as a fierce competitor. Stokes was never one to shy away from a challenge, and he thrived on the intensity of county cricket. The grind of playing day in and day out against some of the best domestic players in England helped him develop the stamina and mental fortitude needed to succeed at the highest level.

While his bowling earned him early praise, it was his batting that would ultimately capture the imagination of fans and pundits alike. Stokes had an attacking style that was rare among young players. He didn't just look to survive at the crease; he looked to dominate. His ability to hit the ball cleanly and with power made him a dangerous prospect in all formats of the game. In many ways, Stokes embodied a new era of cricketer, one who could turn a game on its head with a single spell of bowling or an explosive innings.

Ben Stokes

By 2010, Ben Stokes had made his first-class debut for Durham at the age of 18. It was a momentous occasion for the young cricketer, but it was far from a smooth transition. Stokes' initial foray into first-class cricket was marked by inconsistency, as he struggled to adapt to the rigors of the professional game. While his talent was undeniable, it became clear that raw ability alone wouldn't be enough to succeed at this level. The step up from youth and second XI cricket to the first team was significant, and Stokes found himself battling to prove that he could make an impact on a bigger stage.

Despite these early struggles, there were moments of brilliance that hinted at what was to come. In one of his first appearances for Durham, Stokes scored a century in a County Championship match against Nottinghamshire. It was a sensational performance from a teenager who was still finding his feet in the professional game. The innings showcased Stokes' natural flair with the bat and his ability to seize control of a match. It also sent a clear message to the cricketing world: Ben Stokes was not just another young prospect, he was a player with the potential to do extraordinary things.

Stokes' performances in county cricket quickly caught the attention of England's national selectors. At the time, England was on the lookout for dynamic all-rounders who could bring balance to the team, and Stokes fit the bill perfectly. In 2010, he was selected to represent England in the ICC Under-19 Cricket World Cup. It was his first taste of international cricket, albeit at the junior level, and he didn't disappoint. Stokes was one of the standout performers for England during the tournament, scoring a century against India in the group stage. His aggressive batting and ability to deliver key spells with the ball made him a key figure in the team's campaign.

The Under-19 World Cup was a turning point for Stokes. While England didn't win the tournament, Stokes had announced himself on the global stage. His performances drew widespread praise, and it wasn't long before whispers began circulating about a potential call-up to the senior England side. However, despite his rapid rise through the ranks, Stokes remained grounded. He knew that there was still much work to be done, and that success at the highest level would require more than just flashes of brilliance.

Following the World Cup, Stokes returned to Durham, where he continued to refine his game. The life of a county cricketer can be grueling, with long days spent traveling, training, and playing in often unpredictable English weather. For Stokes, these years were essential to his development. They provided him with the opportunity to learn from experienced players and coaches, and to test himself in a variety of conditions. Whether it was battling against swing in the early-season matches or adjusting to the slower, turning pitches of the later summer, Stokes' time in county cricket was a masterclass in adaptability.

One of the key figures during this period of Stokes' career was Geoff Cook, Durham's head coach. Cook was instrumental in nurturing Stokes' talent, providing him with guidance and mentorship as he navigated the challenges of professional cricket. Under Cook's tutelage, Stokes began to develop a more mature approach to the game. He learned to channel his aggression in more constructive ways, becoming a more disciplined player without losing the fire that made him such a dangerous opponent. Cook's influence extended beyond technical aspects of the game, he also helped Stokes develop the mental resilience that would become one of his defining traits.

By 2011, Stokes had firmly established himself as a key player for Durham. His performances in the County Championship were increasingly consistent, and he was becoming known for his ability to change the course of a match with either bat or ball. Whether it was a quickfire innings to boost his team's total or a crucial spell of bowling that broke through a stubborn partnership, Stokes had the ability to make things happen when his team needed it most. This knack for delivering in pressure situations would later become one of the hallmarks of his career.

Ben Stokes

As his reputation grew, so too did the expectations placed on his shoulders. Stokes was still a young man, and with that came the occasional misstep. There were times when his aggressive style of play led to reckless decisions, both with the bat and ball. He had a tendency to go for big shots when caution was required, or to push for wickets when a more patient approach would have been wiser. These moments of youthful exuberance were frustrating for both Stokes and his coaches, but they were also part of the learning process. Stokes was never the type to shy away from taking risks, and while that sometimes led to failure, it also made him the player he would eventually become.

Off the field, Stokes was adjusting to life as a professional athlete. The pressures of representing a county side, coupled with the growing media attention, were new experiences for the young cricketer. However, Stokes handled these challenges with the same grit and determination that he showed on the pitch. He remained focused on improving his game, always looking for ways to get better. Whether it was working on his bowling action, fine-tuning his batting technique, or improving his fitness, Stokes was relentless in his pursuit of excellence.

While the early years of his county career were marked by growth and development, they were also punctuated by setbacks. Injuries, in particular, were a constant threat. As a fast bowler, Stokes put a tremendous amount of strain on his body, and it wasn't uncommon for him to pick up niggles or more serious injuries that would sideline him for periods of time. These injuries were a source of frustration, but they also taught Stokes valuable lessons about resilience and recovery. He learned how to manage his body better, how to stay fit during long seasons, and how to come back stronger after time away from the game.

Despite these challenges, Stokes' star continued to rise. By 2012, he was being tipped as a future England international, with many predicting that it was only a matter of time before he made his senior debut. His

Ben Stokes

performances for Durham were becoming more consistent, and he was gaining a reputation as one of the most exciting young talents in English cricket. However, there were still hurdles to overcome. Stokes was ambitious, and he knew that success at the county level would not be enough to fulfill his dreams. He wanted to play for England, to test himself against the best in the world, and to prove that he could compete on the biggest stage.

The road to international cricket is never easy, and for Stokes, it was no different. Despite his undeniable talent, there were questions about whether he had the maturity and discipline required to succeed at the highest level. Stokes was known for his fiery temperament, and while that gave him an edge on the field, it also made him prone to moments of indiscipline. There were times when his aggression got the better of him, leading to unnecessary confrontations or poor decisions in the heat.

CHAPTER FOUR: THE INTERNATIONAL BREAKTHROUGH

By 2013, the murmurs of Ben Stokes' undeniable potential had transformed into a roar, and his ascent into the senior England team became inevitable. He had cut his teeth in county cricket, weathering its ups and downs, and was now ready to make his mark on the international stage. While the road to international cricket was one filled with challenges and intense scrutiny, Stokes' journey to wearing the coveted England jersey was one marked by flashes of brilliance, hard-earned lessons, and an unrelenting drive to succeed.

For any cricketer, the call-up to represent their country is a moment of immense pride, but for Stokes, it was also a pivotal moment that would test everything he had worked for. He was brought into the England squad for the 2013-2014 Ashes series in Australia, a trial by fire that would either cement his reputation as a future star or

Ben Stokes

expose the cracks that sometimes appear when young players are thrust into the cauldron of Test cricket. The Ashes, a fiercely contested rivalry between England and Australia, carries a weight of history and expectation, and to make one's debut in such a high-stakes series was a daunting task. Stokes, however, was not one to shy away from the limelight.

England's 2013-2014 Ashes tour in Australia was a baptism of fire for the team as a whole, as they faced a rampant Australian side led by the fearsome pace of Mitchell Johnson and a batting line-up that was both dominant and unyielding. England struggled throughout the series, eventually succumbing to a humiliating 5-0 whitewash. For many, this series would have broken spirits and eroded confidence, but for Ben Stokes, it was the crucible in which he forged his reputation as a player who thrives under pressure and relishes the challenge of adversity.

Stokes made his Test debut in the second match of the series in Adelaide. From the outset, he approached his

Ben Stokes

first international outing with the same fearless attitude that had defined his county cricket. There were no signs of nerves or hesitancy, Stokes looked every bit the part of a player determined to leave his mark. While England struggled collectively, Stokes stood out as a beacon of fight and defiance in a team that was otherwise overwhelmed by the pace and aggression of the Australians. Though his debut match didn't go the way he might have hoped in terms of the result, Stokes' individual performance laid the groundwork for what was to come.

It was in the third Test at Perth where Ben Stokes truly announced himself to the cricketing world. With England facing an uphill battle, Stokes played an innings of extraordinary maturity and power, scoring his maiden Test century. The innings was a revelation, here was a 22-year-old, playing in only his second Test, standing up to one of the most intimidating bowling attacks in the world with poise and authority. Stokes' 120 at the WACA was an innings of controlled aggression, as he took on the likes of Mitchell Johnson and Ryan Harris

Ben Stokes

with an audacity that belied his inexperience at this level. It wasn't just the runs that mattered, it was the way he went about his business. He refused to be intimidated by the occasion, showing a level of mental toughness that few young players possess. The innings was a rare highlight for England in an otherwise bleak series, but for Stokes, it was a career-defining moment that set the tone for his future in Test cricket.

While his century at Perth showcased his batting prowess, Stokes also made an impact with the ball. He took his first five-wicket haul in the fifth and final Test at Sydney, where once again, England were outclassed, but Stokes stood out as a player who was willing to fight until the very end. His figures of 6 for 99 in Australia's first innings were a testament to his skill as an all-rounder. Bowling with pace and aggression, Stokes demonstrated that he could be more than just a useful part-time bowler, he had the potential to be a genuine match-winner with the ball in hand.

Ben Stokes

Despite the crushing defeat that England endured during that Ashes series, Stokes emerged as one of the few positives. The press and pundits alike hailed him as a rare find, a cricketer with the potential to become one of England's greats. His performances, particularly his century at Perth, were widely praised, with many noting that his fearless approach was exactly what England needed in the face of adversity. Stokes had not only survived the brutal initiation of an Ashes tour in Australia, but he had thrived in it, proving that he was ready for the challenges of international cricket.

Following the Ashes, Stokes was seen as a player who could help rejuvenate an England side that was going through a transitional period. His performances in Australia had shown that he was more than just a promising talent, he was a player with the character, skill, and temperament to succeed at the highest level. However, international cricket is unforgiving, and for Stokes, the journey ahead would be far from smooth. The challenges he faced in the years following his Ashes debut would test his resilience, both on and off the field,

Ben Stokes

as he navigated the highs and lows of a career in the public eye.

The next few years saw Stokes continue to develop as an integral part of the England side, though his path was not without its bumps. Injuries, a constant companion for fast bowlers, began to take their toll on his body, and Stokes found himself sidelined at various points. In 2014, during a tour of the West Indies, Stokes fractured his hand in a moment of frustration when he punched a locker after being dismissed cheaply. The injury was a blow, not just physically, but psychologically as well, as it raised questions about his temperament and maturity. It was a reminder that, for all his talent, Stokes was still a young man learning how to cope with the pressures of professional sport.

The setback, however, proved to be a valuable lesson for Stokes. He returned to the England side with a renewed focus, determined to not let his emotions get the better of him. His performances in both Test and One Day International (ODI) cricket continued to impress, as he became a key figure in England's middle order. Stokes' ability to change the course of a match with either bat or ball made him one of the most valuable assets in the team. He was no longer just a promising young cricketer, he was now one of England's most important players.

One of the defining aspects of Ben Stokes' career has been his ability to rise to the occasion in moments of pressure. Time and time again, he has been the player to step up when England needed him most, whether it was with a match-saving innings or a crucial breakthrough with the ball. His mentality on the field is one of relentless aggression and confidence, he plays with the belief that no situation is too daunting, no opponent too strong. It's this mindset that has allowed him to thrive on the international stage, where the pressure is at its highest.

Stokes' development as an international cricketer was further highlighted by his performances in the 2015 home Ashes series against Australia. Playing in front of his home crowd, Stokes once again rose to the challenge,

Ben Stokes

producing a number of match-winning performances that helped England regain the urn. His most memorable contribution came during the fourth Test at Trent Bridge, where he took 6 for 36 in Australia's second innings to seal a comprehensive victory for England. It was another reminder of his ability to deliver in the big moments and cemented his reputation as one of the premier all-rounders in world cricket.

While his exploits in Test cricket continued to make headlines, Stokes was also making waves in the shorter formats of the game. As a dynamic and powerful middle-order batsman, he became a key figure in England's ODI and T20 sides, playing a crucial role in the team's transformation from an underachieving unit to one of the most dominant limited-overs teams in the world. Stokes' ability to clear the boundary with ease and his knack for producing game-changing spells of bowling made him a vital component in England's rise to the top of the ODI rankings.

However, just as Stokes was hitting his stride as an international cricketer, he faced one of the biggest challenges of his career, an off-field controversy that threatened to derail everything he had worked for. In 2017, Stokes was involved in a late-night altercation outside a nightclub in Bristol, which led to his arrest on suspicion of affray. The incident was a major scandal, with Stokes being suspended from the England team pending the outcome of a legal investigation.

The incident was a turning point in Stokes' career and life. He had always played with a fiery temperament, but now that aggression had spilled over off the field, leading to serious consequences. The fallout from the incident was immense, Stokes missed the 2017-2018 Ashes series in Australia, a tour where his absence was keenly felt by England. For months, his future in the England team was uncertain, and there were questions about whether he would ever be able to regain his place.

Stokes, however, is not someone who backs down from a challenge. During this difficult period, he focused on his

Ben Stokes

fitness and worked tirelessly behind the scenes to prepare for his eventual return to the team. When the legal proceedings concluded in 2018, with Stokes being found not guilty of affray, he was welcomed back into the England fold. The experience had been a humbling one, and it had forced Stokes to reflect on his actions and the responsibilities that came with being a high-profile athlete.

CHAPTER FIVE: THE 2019 WORLD CUP AND THE REBIRTH OF A CHAMPION

As the summer of 2019 approached, the cricketing world buzzed with excitement and anticipation for the ICC Cricket World Cup. This tournament was not merely another competition on the calendar; it was a defining moment for English cricket, a chance to break free from decades of underachievement and to finally lay claim to the title of world champions. Ben Stokes, now an established all-rounder, was at the forefront of this endeavor, embodying the hopes and dreams of a nation that longed for cricketing glory.

The pressure on the England team was palpable, especially after their disappointing exit from the previous World Cup in 2015, where they failed to make it past the group stages. The England cricketing community had undergone a radical transformation

Ben Stokes

under the guidance of new coach Trevor Bayliss and captain Eoin Morgan, adopting an aggressive, fearless brand of cricket that had revitalized the team. Stokes, with his dynamic playing style and ability to rise in high-pressure situations, was a perfect fit for this new ethos.

As the tournament approached, England was one of the favorites. The team had a formidable lineup filled with explosive batsmen and a varied bowling attack, but with that favor came the weight of expectation. Stokes, now a key player, was acutely aware of what was at stake. He had experienced the ups and downs of international cricket, and he understood that this World Cup could be his chance to truly etch his name into cricketing history.

The tournament kicked off on May 30, 2019, and England's first match against South Africa was a showcase of the team's intent. England won convincingly, setting the tone for what would become a thrilling and unpredictable tournament. Stokes played a crucial role, contributing both with bat and ball. As the matches progressed, England's form fluctuated. They were dominant at times, but inconsistent performances meant that they were not guaranteed a place in the knockout stages. The pressure began to mount, and Stokes was keenly aware of the scrutiny from fans and the media.

However, it was in the critical matches that Stokes truly came into his own. One of the most memorable moments of the tournament came during England's group-stage clash against Pakistan. In a nail-biting contest, Stokes demonstrated not only his cricketing ability but also his mental fortitude. Chasing a challenging target, England found themselves in a precarious position, and the pressure was immense. Stokes, showing maturity beyond his years, anchored the innings, guiding his team to a dramatic victory. His ability to remain calm under pressure was becoming a hallmark of his playing style, and it was a trait that would serve him well as the tournament progressed.

Ben Stokes

As the tournament moved toward the knockout stages, Stokes' performances became increasingly influential. In the semi-final against Australia, England was faced with the daunting task of overcoming their old rivals. The stakes were higher than ever, and the atmosphere at Edgbaston was electric. The match turned out to be a classic, filled with dramatic twists and turns. Stokes played a critical innings, scoring a vital 89 runs in a tense chase. His ability to absorb pressure and deliver when it mattered most was becoming evident to everyone watching. In what seemed to be a difficult position, he remained undaunted, navigating the complexities of the match with a blend of skill and composure.

With the tension mounting, Stokes found himself in a position that mirrored many of the high-pressure scenarios he had faced before. In a pivotal moment, he executed a brilliant run-out that not only turned the tide but demonstrated his all-around capability. England eventually triumphed over Australia, reaching the final and setting the stage for what would become one of the most dramatic days in cricket history.

On July 14, 2019, the final was set against New Zealand at Lord's, a venue steeped in cricketing history. As the teams lined up, the weight of expectation hung heavy in the air. Stokes, now a central figure in the English side, felt the enormity of the occasion. The match was not just about winning; it was a chance for redemption for English cricket, and Stokes was determined to play his part in delivering a historic moment.

The match began, and New Zealand batted first, posting a respectable total. However, as England began their innings, the pressure intensified. England's batting lineup faltered early on, and the team found themselves in dire straits. The situation was tense, and it seemed as if the dreams of a World Cup victory were slipping away. This is where Stokes truly transformed into a leader on the field. He understood that the team needed someone to take charge, to instill belief in the players, and he rose to that challenge.

Ben Stokes

Stokes played a remarkable innings, one that would be etched in the annals of cricketing history. He scored an unbeaten 84 runs, crafting a partnership with Jos Buttler that rekindled hopes of an English victory. With every boundary and single, Stokes propelled the team forward, exhibiting not only his batting skill but also his innate ability to inspire those around him. The spirit of resilience that characterized his career was on full display, as he weathered the pressure of the moment with grace and determination.

As the game progressed toward its climax, the drama reached fever pitch. England found themselves needing a few runs to clinch the title, but as the tension mounted, so did the stakes. In an extraordinary twist, Stokes found himself at the center of one of the most controversial moments in cricketing history. As he attempted to take a quick single, he inadvertently deflected the ball to the boundary, resulting in six runs being awarded to England. It was a moment that encapsulated the essence of sport—where fortune can change in an instant and where a single action can alter the course of history.

As the final overs unfolded, the weight of the moment bore down on Stokes and the entire England side. With the match hanging in the balance, Stokes stood firm, determined to see his team over the line. In a surreal conclusion, the match ended in a tie, and the World Cup final went to a Super Over for the first time in history. The atmosphere was electric, the stakes higher than ever.

In the Super Over, Stokes once again demonstrated his ability to rise to the occasion. Batting alongside Buttler, he delivered when it mattered most, guiding England to a competitive total. New Zealand, however, was no ordinary opponent, and they responded fiercely, needing to match England's score to force the match into yet another tie. The drama culminated in the final moments as the outcome came down to the last ball. When the dust settled, England was declared the winner based on the boundary count rule, marking a historic moment in cricket.

Ben Stokes

Stokes' performance throughout the match was nothing short of heroic. He had not only anchored the innings but had also shown incredible composure and leadership in the face of adversity. He was named Player of the Match, but more importantly, he had become a national hero overnight. The victory was not just a personal triumph for Stokes; it was a cathartic moment for English cricket, an era of resurgence that signified a new chapter in the sport.

The aftermath of the World Cup saw Stokes elevated to icon status. He was celebrated not only for his cricketing ability but also for the heart and determination he had shown throughout the tournament. His ability to perform under pressure and turn matches around was now a part of cricketing folklore. He was the embodiment of a team that had transformed from perennial underachievers into world champions, and his story resonated with fans far and wide.

Ben Stokes

With the weight of expectation lifted and a World Cup title to his name, Stokes' confidence soared. He had proven himself as a match-winner, a player who could be relied upon in crucial situations. But even as he basked in the glory of victory, he knew that the journey of a cricketer is one filled with challenges. Maintaining excellence in international cricket requires constant adaptation, growth, and learning.

In the following months, Stokes would continue to thrive in the sport, participating in series against various opponents. His performances remained consistent, and he became a key player for England across all formats. Yet, the pressures of international cricket never fully dissipated. As he settled into his role as an established player, Stokes had to navigate the expectations that came with his newfound fame. The world was watching, and he was determined to live up to the expectations of a hero.

Ben Stokes

Stokes' journey to becoming a champion was not merely defined by his cricketing accomplishments. His resilience and character shone through during challenging times, both on and off the field. He was a testament to the notion that true champions are forged in adversity, and they rise stronger than ever after facing their demons. The 2019 World Cup was a pivotal chapter in Stokes' life, one that would forever change the trajectory of his career and solidify his place in the pantheon of cricketing greats.

In the years that followed, Stokes would face further challenges, but he had already demonstrated the spirit of a champion. The lessons he had learned throughout his journey, from the raw talent that emerged in his youth to the victorious moments that defined his international career, had shaped him into not just a cricketer but a beacon of hope and inspiration for aspiring athletes everywhere.

As Stokes reflected on the World Cup victory and the significance it held for him and English cricket, he understood that this was only the beginning. His journey was far from over, and the world awaited more chapters in the story of a cricketer who had defied the odds, battled through adversity, and emerged as a symbol of resilience and triumph. Ben Stokes was not just a player; he was a champion whose legacy would continue to inspire generations to come.

CHAPTER SIX: A LEGACY DEFINED

As Ben Stokes settled into his role as a cricketing hero, the accolades and honors began to pile up. The 2019 World Cup was a defining moment not just for him but for English cricket as a whole. Yet, as the excitement of the victory began to fade, Stokes found himself in a position where he had to reconcile the expectations of a national hero with the realities of professional sports. It was a challenging balancing act that would define his next chapter and ultimately shape his legacy.

The immediate aftermath of the World Cup saw Stokes thrust into the limelight. He became a household name, celebrated not only for his cricketing prowess but also for his larger-than-life persona. His performances had captured the hearts of fans, and he was hailed as the savior of English cricket. Yet, with fame came scrutiny. Every move he made was analyzed, and every mistake was magnified. The pressure to perform weighed heavily on his shoulders, and it was during this period that Stokes would face one of the most challenging times in his career.

The summer following the World Cup brought a series of international fixtures, and Stokes was expected to lead from the front. He had become a linchpin of the England team, and his ability to deliver in high-pressure situations had set a new standard for expectations. Stokes' performances in the subsequent Test series against Australia for the Ashes were pivotal. As a series steeped in history and rivalry, the Ashes brought its own set of pressures, and Stokes was determined to prove that he was more than just a one-time hero.

The series kicked off in August 2019, and the atmosphere was electric. Australia, as always, came into the series as formidable opponents, but Stokes was undeterred. His mindset was clear: he wanted to lead by example and deliver performances that would solidify his place in the pantheon of cricketing greats. As the

Ben Stokes

series unfolded, it became evident that Stokes was ready to embrace the challenge.

The third Test at Headingley became a defining moment for Stokes and would forever be remembered as one of the most remarkable comebacks in cricket history. England found themselves in a dire position, needing 359 runs to win with only a handful of wickets remaining. The odds were stacked against them, and the atmosphere was tense, but Stokes remained focused. He had been in such positions before and knew that all it took was one good partnership to change the tide.

As Stokes walked out to bat, he carried the weight of expectation, not only from his teammates but from a nation that had witnessed his heroics in the World Cup. The crowd at Headingley was electric, filled with anticipation and hope. In those moments, Stokes tapped into the belief that had defined his career, a belief in his ability to overcome adversity and to perform under pressure. The innings that followed was a masterclass in batting, a blend of aggression and calculated risk-taking.

Ben Stokes

With each boundary, Stokes revitalized the hopes of the English crowd. He unleashed a flurry of strokes, punishing any loose deliveries while displaying remarkable footwork and technique. It was a performance that showcased his evolution as a player; he was no longer just a talented all-rounder but a formidable batsman who could change the course of a match single-handedly. Stokes' partnership with Jack Leach became legendary as the two defied expectations, culminating in a nail-biting finish that saw England secure a historic victory.

Stokes finished the innings with an extraordinary 135 not out, and in that moment, he became a symbol of resilience and determination. The Headingley Test would go down in history as one of the greatest comebacks in the sport, and Stokes emerged not just as a match-winner but as a leader. His ability to inspire those around him, to lift the team in their darkest moments, was a quality that set him apart from his contemporaries.

Ben Stokes

Yet, even as Stokes basked in the glory of his performance, he knew that the path to greatness was fraught with challenges. The pressures of being a sports icon can often lead to the darker side of fame, intense scrutiny, expectations, and the inevitable pitfalls that come with public life. For Stokes, this period was not without its challenges. The strain of constant attention began to take its toll on his mental health.

In the months that followed, Stokes experienced moments of self-doubt and anxiety, struggles that he had faced before but were amplified by his newfound fame. The pressure to continuously perform at the highest level weighed heavily on him. Behind the scenes, he battled with his own demons, grappling with the expectations that surrounded him. It was a personal journey that he would navigate privately, understanding that the journey of an athlete is not just about physical prowess but also mental resilience.

In 2020, amidst the global pandemic, the world of cricket was forced to adapt to new realities. The sport, like many others, faced unprecedented challenges as matches were postponed, and the way the game was played changed dramatically. However, this period also provided Stokes with an opportunity for reflection. He took the time to recalibrate, to assess what was truly important in his life. He found solace in family, friends, and the simple joys that life had to offer beyond the cricketing arena.

As cricket slowly returned, Stokes resumed his role as a leader on the field. The absence of crowds during matches changed the dynamics of the game, but it didn't dampen Stokes' spirit. He became a beacon of hope for his teammates, encouraging them to embrace the new challenges that lay ahead. His performances in Test matches and limited-overs cricket continued to impress, and he was determined to use his platform to advocate for mental health awareness.

Stokes became increasingly vocal about the importance of mental health in sports. He recognized that athletes,

Ben Stokes

often seen as invincible, faced pressures that could lead to significant mental health challenges. Through his experiences, he wanted to shine a light on the importance of seeking help and normalizing conversations around mental health. Stokes' willingness to share his struggles resonated with fans and fellow players alike, and it helped foster a culture of openness in a sport that had traditionally shied away from discussing such issues.

As the cricketing world began to stabilize, the international calendar resumed, and Stokes was eager to continue his legacy on the field. His performances in subsequent series further solidified his reputation as one of the game's leading all-rounders. He excelled in various formats, showcasing his versatility and adaptability. Yet, his commitment to the sport went beyond individual performances; Stokes aimed to inspire the next generation of cricketers, sharing his experiences and encouraging young players to embrace their unique journeys.

Ben Stokes

Throughout this period, Stokes continued to engage with his fans, utilizing social media to connect with them. He shared insights into his training regimen, offered glimpses into his life off the field, and engaged in conversations around the sport. This authenticity endeared him to fans, who saw him not just as a cricketer but as a relatable figure navigating the complexities of fame and performance.

As 2021 approached, Stokes had firmly established himself as a modern-day great in the cricketing world. His achievements, both as a player and as a leader, became the benchmarks for aspiring athletes. Yet, even as he embraced the accolades and recognition, he remained grounded. Stokes understood that his journey was ongoing, and that legacy was not merely about titles and records, but about the impact one leaves on others.

In the backdrop of his professional life, Stokes' personal life also flourished. He married his long-time partner, Clare Ratcliffe, and they welcomed their first child, a daughter named Amelia. This new chapter brought him

Ben Stokes

immense joy and perspective. The responsibilities of fatherhood helped him navigate the pressures of professional sports with a renewed sense of purpose. He found himself more focused, driven not just by personal ambition but by the desire to set an example for his daughter.

As Stokes continued to contribute to the England cricket team, he became an integral part of discussions surrounding the future of the sport. His insights and experiences were valued, and he was often sought after for mentorship roles, guiding younger players in their development. This transition from player to mentor marked another evolution in Stokes' career, as he began to understand the importance of legacy beyond personal achievement.

In the midst of this, the cricketing landscape continued to evolve. The introduction of various formats, including T20 leagues, brought about new challenges and opportunities for players. Stokes embraced these changes, participating in global tournaments that allowed him to showcase his skills on international platforms. He quickly became a sought-after player in T20 leagues, but he remained committed to representing England in international competitions.

As Stokes moved forward, his legacy became multifaceted. He was not only remembered for his extraordinary performances on the field but also for his advocacy for mental health, his commitment to youth development, and his genuine passion for the sport. The narrative of Ben Stokes evolved from that of a promising young talent to a seasoned cricketer who had faced and overcome challenges, embodying resilience, leadership, and compassion.

Through it all, Stokes maintained a deep connection to the roots of the game. He often spoke about his early inspirations, the players who had shaped his journey, and the importance of passing that legacy on. He recognized that cricket was not just a sport; it was a community, a culture that needed to be nurtured and preserved. His efforts to engage with fans and promote grassroots

Ben Stokes

cricket reflected this commitment, ensuring that the sport continued to thrive for future generations.

As the years rolled on, Ben Stokes emerged as a global ambassador for cricket. He traveled the world, sharing his story and experiences, and inspiring young athletes to pursue their dreams. Whether it was through coaching clinics, school visits, or public appearances, he was dedicated to giving back to the sport that had given him so much.

CHAPTER SEVEN: THE TRIALS AND TRIUMPHS

Ben Stokes' path to further establish his reputation in the cricket world was not without difficulties. The burden of intense public scrutiny, one's own struggles, and the constant expectation to perform at the highest caliber all came with fame. This chapter explores the experiences that put Stokes to the test on and off the field and helped to mold him into the person he is today.

Being a well-known athlete comes with pressures that are frequently amplified in public. This struck an especially deep chord with Stokes, who was juggling the demands of celebrity with the need to stay true to himself. The September 2017 brawl in Bristol, which would change the course of his career, was one occasion that threw this relationship into stark light. During a night out, the incident happened, and Stokes was caught up in a fight that led to accusations of affray.

Ben Stokes

This incident had immediate and serious repercussions. Stokes' status in the England team for the forthcoming Ashes series was in jeopardy due to his suspension from the team. The incident created a media frenzy, with tabloid headlines questioning his character and speculating about his future. He felt the weight of public opinion strongly; not only was his career on the line, but his reputation as well.

Amid the confusion, Stokes was engaged in a struggle within. He was well aware of the disappointment his actions had created in his family as well as among supporters and teammates. This insight served as a spur to introspection as he tried to figure out what decisions had brought him to that terrible night. He was compelled by the experience to face the less desirable aspects of celebrity and the possible negative effects of being well-known.

Stokes continued to concentrate on establishing his innocence during the ensuing judicial proceedings. He used the trial as an opportunity to publicly admit that he had to accept responsibility for his conduct and to show that he was committed to changing. Even though he was ultimately found not guilty of affray in August 2018, the incident had a lasting impact on his career. Determined to restore his reputation, he entered the cricket pitch with a fresh feeling of purpose.

Stokes found comfort in the cricket community even as the legal struggle persisted. His on-field performance served as a vent for his annoyances and a means of self-reflection. He showed his resilience in the face of adversity by putting up a string of outstanding performances after rejoining the England squad. Stokes saw that cricket was a team sport that necessitated cooperation and trust among teammates, not only about individual achievements.

After everything was said and done, Stokes came away from the experience knowing himself better. Not only as a player but also as a person, he gained greater resilience. His experiences made him more sympathetic to people going through similar difficulties.

Ben Stokes

Reinforcing his commitment to advocate for mental health awareness, he began using his platform to emphasize the importance of seeking help and sharing one's burdens, encouraging others to break the stigma surrounding mental health in sports.

With each passing match, Stokes not only reclaimed his spot in the England lineup but also reinforced his status as a key player. His performances were marked by an intensity and determination that resonated with fans. One particular series that highlighted this was the 2019 Ashes series against Australia. Following his remarkable innings at Headingley, Stokes played a pivotal role in the remaining matches, demonstrating his ability to perform under pressure and rise to the occasion when it mattered most.

The Ashes series was charged with emotion and rivalry, and Stokes became a focal point of England's efforts. In a sport that often hinges on individual moments, Stokes seemed to thrive in the spotlight, harnessing the energy of the crowd and channeling it into his performances. His passionate displays were not just about runs and wickets; they were a reflection of his growth as a leader and an athlete. Stokes had transformed from a promising talent into a seasoned player who understood the intricacies of high-pressure cricket.

As the cricketing calendar moved forward, Stokes continued to face challenges that would test his resolve. The COVID-19 pandemic struck in early 2020, leading to the suspension of sporting events globally. This unprecedented situation forced athletes to adapt to new realities, with matches postponed and training routines disrupted. For Stokes, this period was marked by uncertainty, but it also provided an opportunity for introspection and personal growth.

During the lockdowns, Stokes found solace in family life. He used the time to reconnect with his loved ones and engage in activities outside of cricket. This newfound perspective allowed him to appreciate the small joys in life, reminding him that there was more to existence than cricket alone. As the world gradually reopened, Stokes returned to the field with a renewed sense of purpose and clarity.

The summer of 2020 saw the return of international cricket, albeit under strict health protocols. Stokes' performances were a testament to his resilience; he seamlessly transitioned back into the rigors of competitive cricket, showcasing his versatility in both Test matches and limited-overs formats. He embraced the challenges of playing in empty stadiums, understanding that the essence of the game extended beyond the cheers of the crowd.

Stokes' leadership qualities came to the forefront during this period. With established players taking a back seat due to the pandemic, he stepped into a more prominent role within the England setup. His ability to inspire and motivate younger players became crucial as the team navigated a series of challenges. Stokes understood that leadership was not just about being a star player; it was also about fostering a culture of collaboration, trust, and resilience among teammates.

In the latter part of 2020, Stokes was appointed as the vice-captain of the Test team, a role that signified the faith his peers and management had in him. This position allowed him to contribute to team strategies, mentor emerging talent, and share his experiences. Stokes' approach to leadership was rooted in authenticity; he led by example, encouraging players to express themselves freely and embrace their individuality.

As the new year unfolded, Stokes faced another significant challenge: the demands of international tours amidst a global health crisis. The England team embarked on a tour to India, where conditions would be vastly different from what they were accustomed to. The team faced unique challenges, including stringent bio-secure environments and rigorous testing protocols. Stokes' leadership was essential in navigating these complexities, as he sought to foster a sense of camaraderie among players.

Ben Stokes

In India, Stokes showcased his ability to adapt to different conditions. The series tested not just physical skill but mental fortitude. On challenging pitches, where runs were hard to come by, he led from the front, demonstrating his commitment to the team's success. The tours became a testament to his growth as a player; he was no longer just a talented all-rounder, but a well-rounded cricketer who understood the nuances of the game.

As Stokes continued to rise through the ranks, he remained grounded, always acknowledging the people and experiences that had shaped his journey. He made a concerted effort to give back to the sport that had provided him so much. Stokes engaged with fans, sharing his journey through social media, and encouraging young players to pursue their dreams, no matter the obstacles they faced.

The trials that Stokes faced, both on and off the field, became a vital part of his story. They defined him as

Ben Stokes

much as his achievements. The scrutiny, setbacks, and challenges he encountered added depth to his character, allowing him to connect with fans and aspiring cricketers on a personal level. Stokes understood that his legacy would be shaped not only by the runs he scored or the wickets he took but also by how he handled adversity and inspired others in the process.

CHAPTER EIGHT: A LEGACY IN THE MAKING

As the sun began to set on the cricketing calendar, Ben Stokes found himself at a crossroads, a moment that not only encapsulated his journey thus far but also set the stage for his enduring legacy in the sport. With the achievements and trials that had shaped him, Stokes was no longer just a player; he was a figure emblematic of grit, determination, and transformation. This chapter explores the various elements that contribute to Stokes' legacy, from his impact on the game and its culture to his role as an inspiration for future generations.

Stokes' emergence as a cricketing icon was characterized not only by his remarkable skill set but also by his tenacity in the face of adversity. In many ways, he represented a shift in the culture of cricket, one that embraced a more aggressive style of play, reflecting the evolving nature of the game. The era in which he thrived was marked by explosive batting, dynamic bowling, and an overall approach that celebrated risk-taking. Stokes embodied this evolution, often taking it upon himself to change the course of a game through sheer willpower and talent.

His iconic performances, particularly in high-stakes matches, left an indelible mark on cricket history. One of the most striking examples was the 2019 ICC Cricket World Cup Final, where his extraordinary innings not only propelled England to victory but also showcased the qualities that endeared him to fans worldwide. It was a moment that encapsulated the spirit of modern cricket, intense, unpredictable, and electric. Stokes' ability to thrive under pressure resonated with audiences, and his performances became a touchstone for what it meant to play cricket at the highest level.

Beyond his on-field exploits, Stokes was pivotal in challenging the perceptions surrounding the sport. Traditionally viewed as a gentleman's game, cricket had its share of norms and conventions that often stifled individuality. However, Stokes' unapologetic style and

Ben Stokes

emotional engagement brought a new flavor to the sport. He was not afraid to express his feelings, whether it was celebrating a wicket with raw enthusiasm or allowing the weight of defeat to affect him deeply. This authenticity fostered a connection with fans, particularly younger audiences who were drawn to his relatability.

Stokes' influence extended beyond his personal achievements; he became a beacon of hope for aspiring cricketers. He was a living testament to the idea that resilience could lead to triumph, regardless of the obstacles one faced. Through his journey, he inspired countless young players to dream big and believe in their capabilities. His openness about mental health and the struggles he faced provided a much-needed platform for discussions within the cricket community. Stokes championed the idea that vulnerability is not a weakness; it is a fundamental aspect of being human.

The conversations sparked by Stokes also led to a broader cultural shift within cricket, emphasizing the importance of mental well-being alongside physical performance. His willingness to share his experiences resonated with players across various levels of the sport, prompting organizations to prioritize mental health initiatives. In a high-pressure environment like professional sports, where athletes often feel the burden of expectations, Stokes' advocacy created a safe space for others to voice their challenges.

As he continued to carve his legacy, Stokes also recognized the importance of community. He understood that the sport he loved was built on the collective efforts of players, coaches, and fans. His commitment to giving back was evident in his philanthropic endeavors, as he sought to support grassroots cricket initiatives and programs that aimed to make the sport more accessible to underprivileged youth. Stokes firmly believed in the transformative power of cricket to bring people together, bridging divides and fostering a sense of belonging.

The journey of an athlete often includes a reflection on one's roots. For Stokes, this meant staying connected to his family and the early influences that shaped his love for cricket. His parents played a vital role in nurturing his talent, encouraging him to pursue his passion while also instilling a sense of discipline and resilience. Throughout his career, Stokes acknowledged their sacrifices, and his success became a celebration of not just his hard work, but also the unwavering support of his family.

In examining his legacy, one cannot overlook the impact of leadership on Stokes' journey. After being appointed captain of the Test team, he faced the challenge of guiding a squad through the unpredictable waters of modern cricket. Stokes recognized that effective leadership extended beyond strategic decisions; it was about nurturing a positive team environment where players felt valued and empowered. His approach emphasized inclusivity, collaboration, and trust, fostering a culture where every member of the team felt they could contribute.

Stokes' captaincy style was characterized by its dynamism. He was unafraid to take calculated risks, whether it meant pushing players to perform beyond their limits or making bold tactical choices in matches. This willingness to innovate and challenge norms earned him respect among his peers, as well as the support of fans who appreciated his commitment to an exciting brand of cricket. Stokes became known for leading by example, showcasing not just his skills, but also his unwavering determination to succeed.

As he looked to the future, Stokes was keenly aware of the legacy he was crafting, both for himself and the sport as a whole. He envisioned a cricketing landscape that encouraged diversity, celebrated individuality, and prioritized mental well-being. Stokes recognized that his journey was part of a larger narrative, one that involved uplifting the next generation of cricketers and inspiring them to chase their dreams unapologetically.

The global cricketing community began to take notice of Stokes' efforts. His impact transcended the boundaries of the field, earning him accolades and recognition not only

Ben Stokes

for his playing skills but also for his role as a positive force within the sport. The discussions he sparked about mental health, diversity, and the future of cricket contributed to a richer understanding of the sport's potential as a platform for change.

As this chapter draws to a close, the legacy of Ben Stokes is one of resilience, authenticity, and inspiration. His journey is a testament to the power of perseverance in the face of adversity, reminding us that greatness is not solely defined by achievements but by the values we uphold and the impact we leave on others. With each passing match, Stokes continued to build a legacy that resonated far beyond the boundaries of cricket, encouraging generations to come to embrace their individuality and pursue their passions with unwavering determination.

CHAPTER NINE: THE PINNACLE OF SUCCESS

As Ben Stokes reached the apex of his career, he found himself not only a celebrated athlete but a symbol of determination and resilience. His journey from an aspiring young cricketer to a global sports icon was a story of grit, perseverance, and unrelenting passion for the game. Chapter eight explores the culmination of Stokes' efforts, where his numerous achievements began to define him as one of cricket's all-time greats, and the unique way he embraced the challenges that came with success.

The pinnacle of success in any athlete's career is often marked by a few defining moments that not only etch their names in the annals of history but also encapsulate their entire journey. For Ben Stokes, these moments were abundant, but none more so than his unforgettable performance during the 2019 ICC Cricket World Cup. As England's hopes hung in the balance during the final

Ben Stokes

against New Zealand, it was Stokes who stood tall amidst the chaos. With the world watching, his incredible innings turned what seemed like a lost cause into one of the greatest comebacks in the sport's history. His heroics in that final not only secured England's first-ever World Cup win but also transformed him into a household name. Stokes' performance was not just about skill; it was about mental fortitude, staying calm under pressure, and an indomitable will to win.

The World Cup victory was the ultimate reward for years of hard work, both on and off the field. It was a testament to Stokes' evolution as a cricketer. He had always possessed raw talent, but this victory was the embodiment of experience, wisdom, and maturity. The way he handled the pressure during that final, whether it was taking the game to a Super Over or those crucial six runs from the deflected boundary was the result of years spent honing his game and understanding the finer nuances of cricket.

Ben Stokes

However, the 2019 World Cup was just one of many high points in Stokes' illustrious career. Shortly after his World Cup triumph, he once again demonstrated his brilliance during the 2019 Ashes series. The Headingley Test match, often described as one of the greatest in the history of the sport, saw Stokes produce a match-winning knock that defied belief. With England facing an almost impossible target of 359 runs, and with nine wickets down, Stokes carried the weight of an entire nation on his shoulders. His unbeaten 135 was not just an extraordinary innings, but a display of tenacity and sheer willpower. It was cricket at its finest—a player single-handedly willing his team to victory against all odds.

That Headingley knock was a microcosm of Ben Stokes the cricketer: tough, relentless, and willing to push the boundaries of what was deemed possible. As his bat came down on the final shot that sealed England's win, the cricketing world stood in awe. It was the kind of innings that legends are made of, and for many, it

Ben Stokes

solidified Stokes' place among cricket's pantheon of greats.

But success, as Stokes knew well, brought with it its own set of challenges. Being at the top meant that every move was scrutinized, every decision weighed, and the expectations were higher than ever before. As his fame and success grew, so did the pressures associated with them. Stokes was no longer just a cricketer; he was a role model, a public figure, and a global ambassador for the sport. His actions, both on and off the field, were now under constant surveillance, and maintaining a balance between personal and professional life became increasingly challenging.

Stokes, however, was never one to shy away from responsibility. Instead of letting the pressures consume him, he embraced them. He understood that with success came the responsibility of guiding the next generation of cricketers. He began taking a more active role in mentoring young players, sharing his experiences and helping them navigate the complexities of international cricket. Whether it was offering advice to a rookie fast bowler or sharing tips on handling pressure during crunch moments, Stokes had evolved into a leader in the truest sense.

As his stature in the cricketing world grew, so did the accolades. Stokes began collecting awards and honors, from being named the ICC Player of the Year to winning multiple domestic and international cricketing awards. His influence extended beyond England; he was now a global figure, admired by fans and players alike across different cricketing nations. He was no longer just a player; he was an icon, someone whose name was mentioned alongside cricketing legends like Sir Ian Botham, Sachin Tendulkar, and Brian Lara.

Stokes' success on the field also led to opportunities off it. He became a brand ambassador for various companies, using his platform to not only promote products but also causes close to his heart. Whether it was mental health awareness, supporting grassroots cricket, or championing diversity in sports, Stokes used his influence to drive positive change. He was acutely aware of the power he wielded as a public figure and was determined to use it for the greater good.

However, amidst the glitz and glamour of success, Stokes never lost sight of who he was. He remained grounded, rooted in the values instilled in him by his family and his upbringing in New Zealand. Fame and fortune had not changed the core of Ben Stokes. He was still the hardworking, passionate, and fiercely competitive player who lived for the game of cricket. His teammates often spoke of his humility and how, despite his success, Stokes remained approachable and supportive, always putting the team first.

As Stokes continued to play at the highest level, he also began reflecting on his legacy. What kind of cricketer did he want to be remembered as? What impact did he want to leave on the game? These were questions that started to occupy his mind as he entered the latter stages of his career. For Stokes, it wasn't just about the runs he scored or the wickets he took; it was about the

Ben Stokes

relationships he built, the lives he touched, and the inspiration he provided to the next generation.

One of the key aspects of Stokes' legacy is his role in changing the perception of what it means to be a modern cricketer. In a sport often steeped in tradition, Stokes represented a new era, an era where passion, emotion, and authenticity were celebrated. He was unapologetically himself, whether he was in the heat of battle on the cricket field or in front of the cameras during press conferences. Stokes showed the world that you could be vulnerable, that you could make mistakes, and that, ultimately, it was how you responded to those mistakes that defined you.

As the chapter on the pinnacle of his career closes, it's clear that Ben Stokes' journey was far from over. He still had much to offer to the sport he loved so dearly. Whether through his leadership, his mentorship, or his performances on the field, Stokes continued to shape the future of cricket. For fans around the world, his name

Ben Stokes

became synonymous with brilliance, resilience, and an unwavering commitment to excellence.

Stokes' success was a reflection of his character, the culmination of years of dedication, sacrifice, and perseverance. It was a reminder to all aspiring cricketers that the road to greatness was never easy, but with hard work and a strong belief in oneself, anything was possible. As Ben Stokes stood at the pinnacle of success, he didn't just rest on his laurels. Instead, he looked ahead, ready to embrace the next challenge, knowing that the journey was just as important as the destination.

CHAPTER TEN: THE WEIGHT OF EXPECTATIONS

By the time Ben Stokes entered this phase of his career, the weight of expectations had become a constant companion. From the passionate fans who lived and breathed cricket, to the media who scrutinized every move, and the international cricketing community that held him to the highest standards, Stokes found himself shouldering more than just the responsibility of his own performance. He carried the aspirations of a nation, and the expectations often came with an immense pressure that could make or break even the most seasoned athletes.

Stokes had already accomplished extraordinary feats in cricket by this point. His heroic performances in the 2019 Cricket World Cup and the Ashes series had placed him at the pinnacle of international cricket. Yet, with every new season, every new tournament, came the unavoidable question: Could he continue to live up to the ever-increasing expectations? For an athlete who had achieved what many considered the height of success, sustaining that level of brilliance was an entirely different challenge.

As a figurehead of English cricket, Stokes was often seen as the man who could change the course of a game single-handedly. This expectation wasn't just built on his undeniable skills but on the emotional investment he had sparked in fans and teammates alike. Cricket fans adored him for his aggression, his fight, and his never-say-die attitude, but this admiration also came with the assumption that Stokes would always rise to the occasion. Whether it was a tight chase, a collapsing middle-order, or the need for a game-changing spell, the question on everyone's mind was always: Where is Stokes? Can he save the day?

This expectation, while a mark of respect, also brought about a unique form of pressure. To some extent, Stokes thrived under it. The pressure seemed to sharpen his focus, push him to new limits, and fuel his performances.

Ben Stokes

But at times, even for someone as mentally tough as Stokes, the burden could be overwhelming. Every athlete, no matter how great, has moments of doubt, and for Stokes, there were periods when the weight of expectation began to feel heavy.

Unlike earlier in his career, where the pressure was mostly internal, stemming from his desire to prove himself, this new kind of pressure came from external sources. It was the scrutiny of the public, the unrelenting media attention, and the knowledge that his performances could make or break England's fortunes. In many ways, it was a natural consequence of greatness; the more Stokes achieved, the more he was expected to achieve.

As he matured, Stokes understood the fine line between using that pressure as motivation and letting it consume him. He became more self-aware, recognizing the need to manage not just his physical training but also his mental and emotional well-being. He acknowledged that maintaining his own mental health was essential to continuing his career at the highest level. To this end, Stokes sought support from sports psychologists and learned to compartmentalize the various pressures he faced, focusing on what he could control and learning to let go of the rest.

The role of captaincy amplified these challenges. When he was handed the reins as England's Test captain, Stokes became the face of the team not just on the field but off it as well. Leading a national side came with its own set of unique pressures. Every tactical decision, every selection, and every post-match interview carried significant weight. The expectations of not only delivering individually but also inspiring and guiding a team compounded the already heavy burden on his shoulders.

Yet, Stokes was not one to shy away from responsibility. His leadership was built on the same principles that had guided his playing career: resilience, determination, and an unyielding belief in his team. As captain, Stokes understood that managing expectations was not just

Ben Stokes

about his own performance but about fostering a culture within the team that could handle the intense scrutiny and pressure that came with playing at the highest level.

One of Stokes' greatest strengths as captain was his ability to lead by example. He didn't ask his players to do anything he wouldn't do himself. Whether it was batting in tough conditions, bowling long spells, or fielding in crucial positions, Stokes demonstrated what it meant to give everything for the team. His teammates often spoke of his tireless work ethic and how his presence in the dressing room lifted the entire squad. It wasn't just his runs or wickets that mattered; it was the energy, intensity, and leadership that he brought to every game.

However, Stokes' leadership style was also marked by empathy. Having faced his own personal and professional struggles, he was acutely aware of the pressures that came with international cricket. He made it a point to check in with his teammates, offering support and understanding when they faced difficulties.

Ben Stokes

Whether it was a young player finding his feet or an experienced campaigner going through a tough patch, Stokes always had time to offer words of encouragement or lend a sympathetic ear. He understood that the weight of expectations could crush even the most talented players, and he sought to create an environment where his teammates could thrive despite the immense pressure.

As Stokes' career progressed, he became more attuned to the realities of fame and success. He understood that cricket fans, and the media, could be fickle; they loved to build heroes, but they also loved to tear them down. One bad performance could overshadow a string of match-winning contributions, and the very fans who once celebrated him could turn critical in a moment. But this reality didn't deter Stokes. If anything, it made him more resolute. He accepted that this was part of the game and that his focus had to remain on what he could control, his preparation, his performance, and his attitude.

Ben Stokes

It wasn't just cricket fans who placed enormous expectations on Stokes; he placed them on himself. Having achieved so much in his career, he constantly pushed himself to get better, to add new dimensions to his game, and to continue being a difference-maker for England. He knew that staying at the top required continuous improvement, and he embraced this challenge with the same enthusiasm that had fueled his rise to stardom.

But even for someone as mentally tough as Stokes, the weight of expectations wasn't always easy to carry. There were moments of doubt, moments where the burden seemed too heavy. The pressures of international cricket, coupled with the responsibilities of leadership, could be overwhelming. Yet, in these moments of difficulty, Stokes often found strength in those around him, his family, his teammates, and his close circle of friends. They provided the support and perspective he needed to keep going, reminding him that while the expectations of the world might be enormous, what mattered most was staying true to himself.

Ben Stokes

As Stokes reflected on his journey, he realized that the weight of expectations was both a blessing and a curse. It pushed him to heights he never thought possible, but it also tested his resolve in ways few could understand. Yet, through it all, Stokes remained unshaken in his love for the game. Cricket was his passion, his calling, and he knew that as long as he played, the expectations would follow. But rather than seeing them as a burden, Stokes chose to view them as a privilege, after all, they were a testament to everything he had achieved.

Ultimately, the weight of expectations became part of Ben Stokes' legacy. It was the price of greatness, the inevitable consequence of being one of the best. But for Stokes, it was never about living up to other people's expectations; it was about constantly challenging himself, pushing his limits, and playing the game with the same passion and intensity that had defined his career from the very beginning.

CHAPTER ELEVEN: THE LEGACY BEGINS TO FORM

As Ben Stokes approached the twilight years of his career, a new narrative began to form, one not just of performances and achievements, but of legacy. A legacy is not built overnight; it's the sum of everything a player contributes to the game, and in Stokes' case, his legacy was becoming multi-faceted. The question on everyone's mind wasn't just what more he could achieve on the field, but what kind of lasting imprint he would leave on the game itself. For an athlete of Stokes' caliber, the end of his playing days wasn't simply a countdown to retirement; it was the gradual unveiling of a story that would resonate for generations.

To fully appreciate the legacy Ben Stokes was beginning to leave, one first had to look at the ripple effect he had on those around him. Younger players, many of whom had grown up watching Stokes' incredible exploits on the field, now had the opportunity to share the dressing room

Ben Stokes

with him. His leadership, not only as a captain but as a senior figure within the team, extended beyond tactical decisions or motivating speeches. Stokes led by example in everything he did, from the way he trained to the relentless passion he displayed in every match. For many young cricketers, simply being around Stokes had a profound impact on how they approached the game. He was a living reminder of what it took to succeed at the highest level, but also of the importance of resilience, commitment, and sheer love for the sport.

In many ways, Stokes' influence on the next generation of cricketers could be considered one of his most enduring legacies. Players looked up to him not only for his obvious talent but also for his ability to handle pressure, his commitment to fitness, and his determination to rise above personal challenges. It's easy to admire someone for their on-field heroics, but what truly set Stokes apart was the way he approached the game holistically. He made it clear that talent alone wasn't enough; it took discipline, mental toughness, and the willingness to constantly evolve. These lessons became part of his legacy, passed down to every cricketer who came through the England ranks during his time.

Another key aspect of Stokes' legacy was the way he redefined the role of the modern cricketer. Traditionally, cricket has often been seen as a game of specialists, batsmen, bowlers, wicketkeepers, each with a clearly defined role. Stokes, however, shattered this mold, proving that a player could excel in all facets of the game. As an all-rounder, he was not only able to contribute with both bat and ball but did so at an elite level. It's one thing to be a decent batsman who bowls occasionally or a bowler who chips in with useful runs, but Stokes elevated both aspects of his game to world-class standards. In doing so, he inspired a new generation of cricketers who aspired to be more than just specialists.

For many aspiring players, Stokes became the blueprint for what a modern cricketer should be: versatile, aggressive, adaptable, and mentally tough. His ability to perform in all formats of the game Test cricket, One-Day Internationals, and T20s meant that he was not pigeonholed into one particular style. Instead, Stokes thrived in every environment, whether it was the grind of a five-day Test or the high-octane pressure of a World Cup final. This versatility became another cornerstone of his legacy, as players coming through the ranks sought to emulate his ability to excel across all formats of the game.

Stokes also had a profound impact on the evolution of England's cricketing culture. For years, English cricket had been criticized for being too cautious, too conservative in its approach, particularly in Test matches. Stokes, along with a few other key figures, played a significant role in transforming the team's mentality. Under his influence, England adopted a more aggressive, fearless style of play, particularly in the longer format. Stokes was never one to settle for a draw or play it safe. His philosophy was that cricket was a game to be won, and this mindset became infectious within the team. England began to play with more freedom, taking more risks, and adopting a bolder approach to Test cricket.

This shift in mentality had a lasting impact on English cricket. Younger players were encouraged to play with more aggression, to trust their instincts, and to embrace the idea that success in cricket wasn't just about defense but about pushing the boundaries of what was possible. Stokes' influence extended beyond just his performances; it was his attitude toward the game that helped reshape England's identity on the global stage. The England team became known for playing with a sense of fearlessness, and this change in culture was one of the most significant aspects of Stokes' legacy.

Beyond his contributions on the field, Stokes' legacy was also shaped by his openness and vulnerability. In a sport where mental toughness is often emphasized to the point where vulnerability is seen as weakness, Stokes

took a different approach. He was open about his struggles with mental health, and in doing so, he became

Ben Stokes

a powerful advocate for mental well-being in the sporting world. When he took a break from cricket to prioritize his mental health, it was a bold move that sent ripples through the sport. It wasn't just about him stepping away, it was a statement that mental health matters, even for athletes at the top of their game.

Stokes' decision to step away, reflect, and seek help showed a level of strength that went beyond physical prowess. It highlighted the importance of taking care of oneself, both mentally and emotionally, and it sparked a broader conversation about mental health in cricket and sport in general. For younger players, seeing someone of Stokes' stature openly discuss his challenges made it easier to seek help when they needed it. In this way, Stokes' legacy wasn't just about cricket—it was about creating an environment where athletes could be human, where they could acknowledge their struggles and seek support without fear of stigma or judgment.

As Stokes continued to play and contribute to the game, his legacy also began to take shape in other arenas. He became an ambassador for cricket, not just in England but globally. His story of rising from adversity, his resilience in the face of personal and professional challenges, and his ability to perform under pressure resonated with fans around the world. Stokes was more than just a cricketer, he was a symbol of perseverance, a figure who embodied the idea that success is not just about talent but about overcoming the obstacles life throws your way.

His legacy was also built on the relationships he fostered with his teammates, coaches, and fans. Stokes was known for his humility off the field, always willing to take time for supporters, sign autographs, and engage with the next generation of cricket lovers. Despite his success, he remained grounded, and this humility endeared him to fans not just in England but around the cricketing world. In an era where sports stars often seem distant and unreachable, Stokes was relatable, someone who wore his heart on his sleeve and played the game with the same passion that fans felt from the stands.

Ben Stokes

As his career began to wind down, thoughts naturally turned to what Stokes would do after he hung up his boots. There was little doubt that he would remain involved in the game in some capacity. Whether as a coach, a commentator, or a mentor, Stokes had too much to offer cricket to simply walk away. His insights into the game, his experience, and his leadership qualities meant that his post-playing career would likely be just as impactful as his time on the field.

The legacy of Ben Stokes was already taking shape before his final ball was bowled. It was a legacy built on more than just runs and wickets; it was built on the way he played the game, the way he led his teams, and the way he inspired those around him. As the curtain slowly began to fall on his playing days, the cricketing world knew that while Stokes' career might come to an end, his legacy would live on for generations to come. In every young cricketer who dreams of hitting a match-winning century or taking a vital wicket in a final, there will be a little bit of Ben Stokes.

Printed in Great Britain
by Amazon